CONTENTS

MW00446431

NOTE ABOUT THE VOL. 16 CDs -- There are FOUR CDs wit

Both CD#1 and CD#2 include SLOWER and FASTER t

It is recommended that you start with the slower tempo CDs and then to move onto th

Tunes included in VOLUME 16 are:

Any codas (⊕) that appear will be played only once on the recording at the end of the last recorded chorus.

PLAY-A-LONG CD INFORMATION

STEREO SEPARATION: LEFT CHANNEL=Bass & Drums; RIGHT CHANNEL=Piano & Drums -- **TUNING NOTES:** Concert Bb & A (A=440)

PERSONNEL ON PLAY-A-LONG RECORDING

JAMEY AEBERSOLD, DAN HAERLE - Piano; JOHN CLAYTON, JOHN GOLDSBY, RUFUS REID,
STEVE RODBY - Bass; MIKE HYMAN, JOHN CLAY, JONATHAN HIGGINS - Drums

Published by
JAMEY AEBERSOLD JAZZ®
P.O. Box 1244
New Albany, IN 47151-1244
www.jazzbooks.com
ISBN 978-1-56224-171-1

Engraving
BENNY HANCOCK & PETE GEARHART

Original Cover Concept
PETE GEARHART

Cover Design
JASON A. LINDSEY

BOOK ONLY: $5.95 U.S.

SUGGESTIONS FOR VARIOUS RECORDED TRACKS

1   PLAIN OLD TURNAROUND No. 1

This is probably the simplest of all turnarounds because it stays in one key throughout each eight bar phrase. The C major scale (concert key) may be played through the first seven bars and will sound fine. In order to effectively lead to the second eight bars you should change key on the 8th measure (II/V7) leading to the new major key of Db (concert). See if you can play through the seventh and eighth bars of the first phrase and then without breaking your melodic phrase, play into several bars of the next phrase.

You may apply any II/V7 patterns you know in the 2, 4, 6, and 8th bars of each line.

2   TURNAROUNDS No. 2

This turnaround is probably the second most common in jazz and pop music. It is possible to play the F (concert) major scale throughout the first eight bars even though there are harmonic clashes. The root movement coupled with the dominant 7th chords moving in fourths seems to allow the soloist much freedom.

Experiment with using a minor II chord/scale in the 2, 4, and 6th bars. Even though the piano player on the record is playing a dominant 7th, you, the soloist, can play a minor and if you connect your lines together it will sound good.

The most important notes to hit are the 3rd and 7th of the dominant 7th's. *See the musical example of this track in this book.*

Try playing the Blues scale across an eight bar phrase for variety. Always use the blues scale that corresponds to the tonic key. For example, the first line would employ the F concert blues scale.

3   TURNAROUND No. 3

This turnaround is often used in jazz songs to add variety. Piano players may throw it in once or twice in a song just to break the monotony of the usual harmonic sequences. You have to be listening to catch it.

A tune like Half Nelson by Miles Davis uses it consistently. *See the two pages of musical examples.*

The 4th tone of the fourth chord/scale is *usually* raised a half step, but not always.

4   TURNAROUNDS No. 4

This turnaround uses the half-diminished chord, minor chords and altered dominants. It may take a little practice to get the true sound of this track flowing through your instrument. This track is quite different than number 1. See the musical examples and play them over and over before attempting to transpose them to other keys. Make sure you have the sound of the turnaround in your head before you begin taking chances. You may want to just listen to the track and sing along with it, occasionally playing notes on your instrument to see where you are in relation to the music.

The dominant 7th chord/scales which occur may be either V7+9 (diminished whole tone), or V7b9 (diminished scale). The two are interchangeable and players slip back and forth from one to the other. The improvised line may not always align (be in harmonic agreement) precisely with the written chord/scale symbol. The restless nature of the dominant 7th chord/scale allows this interesting phenomena.

Don't take this track lightly. It is used often in jazz literature.

5   BALLAD II/V7/I

This track is a workout in II/V7/I using three different but related approaches. The first section is plain old II/V7/I in major. The second section is a little different...the major chord is turned into a minor chord, but the II/V7 remains the same. The end result is II/V7/I-. The third section is the standard minor II/V7/I- using the half-diminished, diminished whole-tone, and minor chord/scales.

If you have practiced with Volume 3, The II/V7/I Progression, you are probably familiar with the third section even though the chords here don't last as long as they do on Volume 3.

This track is interesting as it exposes the soloist and lets him or her get a true look at themselves. Make sure you know these scales: half-diminished, diminished whole-tone, and minor.

When the minor chord/scale appears you should experiment with using substitute scales such as melodic minor, harmonic minor or any other listed in the Scale Syllabus.

6   CYCLES No. 1, 2, 3, 4 & 5

Dominant seventh chord/scales are often the hardest to make any sense out of when trying to play melodically. They seem to pull us back to the roots, 3rd's and 5th's. One way to loosen up the sound is to substitute a minor for the dominant. For example, use G- instead of C7, use C- instead of F7, etc. Since the two scales contain the same notes this substitution is common and it usually sounds fine.

The fourth note of the dominant 7th has much tension and needs to be handled with care.

Experiment with substituting an altered dominant scale right before resolving to the next chord. Learn how to use b9's, #9's, #4's and #5's as tension tones just before resolving to new scale/chord. Examine transcribed solos to see how the masters do it.

7   V7 + 9/I (1 bar each)

This track uses the scale that is so prevalent in jazz - diminished whole-tone. The main point to keep in mind is to resolve smoothly to the major or minor chord/scale. People will often play a nice phrase over the dim. Whole-tone but fail to resolve smoothly. This gives the entire phrase a choppy sound. Since the dim. Whole-tone scale has a lot of tension built into it, you need to spend some time working with each tone of the scale and learn how that tone wants to resolve to a note in the major or minor scale. The scales are related and we need to learn the relationship of one series of tones resolving to another series of tones. I suggest looking into the exercises in Volume 3, The II/V7/I Progressions.

Experiment with substituting an altered dominant scale right before resolving to the next chord. Learn how to use b9, #9, #5 and #4 tones during the first bar and gradually let them resolve to scale tones of the second bar. Do it over and over so your mind's ear can begin to **hear** it. **Be patient**. This is not an easy track.

8   II/V7/I (five different tracks)

Basically each of these tracks lets you practice and solo through all twelve keys, two beats per II/V7 and one bar on the major. This type sequence is very common in jazz tunes.

The jazz musician has to become so familiar with II/V7 in all keys that it becomes a part of him or her and he or she can respond to any II/V7 just as easily as walking or eating. Believe me, it will become that easy if you work at it little by little.

I strongly suggest playing these tracks for background music, letting your mind sing along with the cassette or CD.

Get so you can hear II/V7 and II/V7/I on the radio, TV, movies, concerts, or wherever it is played. It is an important part of our musical heritage and we must learn to identify it and work with it if we ever hope to produce meaningful music.

9   COLTRANE CHANGES

Coltrane changes are built on the first several chords to Giant Steps. John Coltrane used this harmonic sequence in different settings. He would use it as a substitute harmonic section for a standard song of the harmonic basis of a new tune. When it first appeared it seemed very difficult to play long, flowing phrased through the shifting root progressions. After John Coltrane recorded several albums which employed these changes the jazz musician audience began the *hear* the harmonic flow and the next thing we knew, it was part of the jazz vocabulary.

This track and Coltrane Blues will give you an opportunity to explore what was first written and recorded over twenty years ago.

I suggest practicing without the recording for awhile. Begin with playing the triad, 7th, 9th chords then the first 5 notes of the scale, the full scale. Then try to make a phrase that will flow through one bar, then two bars, then three bars, then all four. Take it slowly and make sure you are *hearing* the *root movement* and *quality* of each chord.

This is another track that I strongly recommend singing with before you begin to play. Eventually, we want to be able to play instantly what we are singing in our minds.

10   TURNAROUNDS FINAL

This track is similar to the first section of "I'm Getting Sentimental Over You." I use this harmonic sequence because it seems to sum up the previous tracks which deal with turnarounds, cycles and II/V7's. Like the other track, this one goes through all twelve keys.

You may want to being by playing the roots. Then, gradually work your way into playing the triad, 7th & 9th chords. Try playing the first 5 notes of each scale. Then play the entire scale. You may have to do this without using the recording.

On the V7 + 9 scales see if you can emphasize the tension tones and then resolve convincingly to the next scale/chord.

Again, sing with this track and play it for background music.

11   Bb RHYTHM CHANGES

I have rhythm changes on several of the other play-a-long recordings but none are at this slower tempo.

Some people love to play rhythms changes and others seem to hate playing them. I suspect that those who hate them probably are frustrated because they run out of things to do. To them the changes seem to confine them rather than offer unlimited possibilities.

There are several ways to play on rhythm changes. You can play bebop, in which you plainly outline each and every change, playing standard cliches and licks that came from that era. You can play the Blues scale across the A sections of the tune. Or you can use the bebop approach coupled with Blues, substitute changes and outside playing.

When playing outside or using substitute changes the important thing is to tip in at the 5th and 1st bar or the phrases. By tipping in you let the rhythm section know that you know where you are and it also offers a sense of confirmation to the listener in the audience.

Several substitute chord progressions for the first eight bars are listed below. These are in concert Bb.

1. / F#- B7 / E- A7 / D- G7 / C- F7 / Bb Bb7 / Eb7 E°7 / D- G7 / C- F7 //

2. / F#7 B7 / E7 A7 / D7 G7 / C7 F7 / Bb7 / Eb7 / D7 G7 / C7 F7 //

3. / Bb   Db7 / Gb   A7 / D   F7 / Bb7 / etc. This is Coltrane changes.

4. / Bb7 Ab7 / Gb7 F7 / Bb7 Ab7 / Gb7 F7 / F- Bb7 / Eb Ab7 / D- G7 / C- F7 // This is called "C.T.A."

5. / Bb7 B7 / Bb7 B7 / Bb7 B7 / Bb7 B7 / Bb7 / Eb7 / D- G7 / C- F7 // favorite Horace Silver device.

6. / A- D7 / Ab- D7 / G- C7 / F#- B7 / Bb7 / etc.

7. / Bb G- / C- F7 / ♪·/ ♪·/ ♪·/ ♪·//

12   COLTRANE BLUES

This is a blues based on the Coltrane changes which were introduced on Side 3, Track 6. This is a Bb Blues and it uses the descending II/V7 chords and the Tritone Substitute. The descending II/V7 are in bars 6, 7, 8 &9 and the tritone substitute is located in bars 9 and 10. The last two bars (turnaround) is the Coltrane changes turnaround. The first four bars are also the Coltrane changes leading you into the fifth bar of the blues.

You may want to work on this tune in section...first five bars, bars 5, 6, 7, 8 & 9, the tritone substitute in bars 9 and 10, and finally the turnaround in bars 11 and 12. Piece this tune together slowly. Make sure you can hear the root movements in all the measures, not just a few. Try singing the roots with the recording.

13   SOME OF THE THINGS I AM

This is a complete reworking of the harmonies to the jazz standard, All the Things You Are. The most obvious substitute is the Tritone Substitute. I use it in bars 3, 4, 6, 11, 12, 14, 18, 22, 27, 28 & 34.

The challenge of this progression is to play melodically through the constantly moving harmonies. If you have a grasp of what has been covered up to here, you should have a good start.

Experiment with using melodic minor and harmonic minor scales whenever a minor chord/scale is sounded for one bar. You may also want to play lydian scales when the major chord/scales appear.

14   GUESS WHAT KEY I'M IN

This is an exercise in Coltrane Changes, ascending II/V7's and cycles. See if you can figure out what key it really is in.

NOTE: Half-diminished chord/scales can be thought of as having the same notes as a Major Scale whose root lies a half-step above the root of the half-diminished chord/scale. For instance: Bø (half-diminished) is the same series of tones as the C major scale. Aø is the same as the Bb Major scale. This way of thinking is sometimes helpful in gaining scales and chords.

THE SCALE SYLLABUS

LEGEND: H = Half Step, W = Whole Step; $\triangle$ = Major 7th; $\triangle$ = Major 7th; + or # = raise H; b or – = lower H; Ø = Half-diminished; –3 = 3H (Minor Third)

CHORD/SCALE SYMBOL	SCALE NAME	WHOLE & HALF STEP CONSTRUCTION	SCALE IN KEY OF C	BASIC CHORD IN KEY OF C
FIVE BASIC CATEGORIES				
C	Major	W W H W W W H	C D E F G A B C	C E G B D
C7	Dominant 7th (Mixolydian)	W W H W W H W	C D E F G A Bb C	C E G Bb D
C–	Minor (Dorian)	W H W W W H W	C D Eb F G A Bb C	C Eb G Bb D
CØ	Half Diminished (Locrian)	H W W H W W W	C Db Eb F Gb Ab Bb C	C Eb Gb Bb
C°	Diminished (8 tone scale)	W H W H W H W H	C D Eb F Gb Ab A (Bb) C	C Eb Gb A (Bbb)
1. MAJOR SCALE CHOICES	**SCALE NAME**	**W & H CONSTRUCTION**	**SCALE IN KEY OF C**	**BASIC CHORD IN KEY OF C**
C△ (Can be written C)	Major (don't emphasize the 4th)	W W H W W W H	C D E F G A B C	C E G B D
C△	Major Pentatonic	W W –3 W –3	C D E G A C	C E G B
C△+4	Lydian (major scale with +4)	W W W H W W H	C D E F# G A B C	C E G B D
C△	Bebop (Major)	W W H W H H W H	C D E F G G# A B C	C E G B D
C△b6	Harmonic Major	W W H W H –3 H	C D E F G Ab B C	C E G B D
C△+5, +4	Lydian Augmented	W W W W H W H	C D E F# G# A B C	C E G# B D
C	Augmented	–3 H –3 H –3 H	C D# E G Ab B C	C E G B D
C	6th Mode of Harmonic Minor	–3 H –3 H H H	C D# E F# G A Bb C	C E G B D
C	Diminished (begin with H step)	H W H W H W H W	C Db D# E F# G A Bb C	C Eb Gb Bb (D#)
C	Blues Scale	–3 W H H –3 W	C Eb F F# G Bb C	C E G Bb
2. DOMINANT 7th SCALE CHOICES	**SCALE NAME**	**W & H CONSTRUCTION**	**SCALE IN KEY OF C**	**BASIC CHORD IN KEY OF C**
C7	Dominant 7th	W W H W W H W	C D E F G A Bb C	C E G Bb D
C7	Major Pentatonic	W W –3 W –3	C D E G A C	C E G Bb D
C7	Bebop (Dominant)	W W H W W H H H	C D E F G A Bb B C	C E G Bb D
C7b9	Spanish or Jewish scale	H –3 H W H W W	C Db E F G Ab Bb C	C E G Bb D
C7+4	Lydian Dominant	W W W H W H W	C D E F# G A Bb C	C E G Bb D
C7b6	Hindu	W W H W H W W	C D E F G Ab Bb C	C E G Bb D
C7+ (has +4 & +5)	Whole Tone (6 tone scale)	W W W W W W	C D E F# G# Bb C	C E G# Bb D
C7b9 (also has +9 & +4)	Diminished (begin with H step)	H W H W H W H W	C Db D# E F# G A Bb C	C E G Bb D
C7+9 (also has b9,+4,+5)	Diminished Whole Tone	H W H W W W W	C Db D# E F# G# Bb C	C E G#/Ab Bb D (D#)
C7	Blues Scale	–3 W H H –3 W	C Eb F F# G Bb C	C E G Bb D
DOMINANT 7th SUSPENDED 4th				
C7 sus 4	MAY BE WRITTEN	W W H W W H W	C D E F G A Bb C	C F G Bb D
C7 sus 4	G–C	W W –3 W –3	Bb C D F G	C F G Bb D
C7 sus 4		W W H W W H W	C D E F G A Bb C	C F G Bb D
3. MINOR SCALE CHOICES*	**SCALE NAME**	**W & H CONSTRUCTION**	**SCALE IN KEY OF C**	**BASIC CHORD IN KEY OF C**
C– or C–7	Minor (Dorian)	W H W W W H W	C D Eb F G A Bb C	C Eb G Bb D
C– or C–7	Pentatonic (Minor Pentatonic)	–3 W W –3 W	C Eb F G Bb C	C Eb G Bb D
C– or C–7	Bebop (Minor)	W H H H W W W H	C D Eb E F G A Bb C	C Eb G Bb D
C–△ (maj. 7th)	Melodic Minor (ascending)	W H W W W W H	C D Eb F G A B C	C Eb G B D
C– or C–6 or C–△	Harmonic Minor	W H W W H –3 H	C D Eb F G Ab B C	C Eb G B D
C– or C–7	Diminished (begin with W step)	W H W H W H W H	C D Eb F Gb Ab A B C	C Eb Gb Bb
C–△ (b6 & maj. 7th)	Blues Scale	–3 W H H –3 W	C Eb F F# G Bb C	C Eb G B D
C– or C–b9b6	Phrygian	H W W W H W W	C Db Eb F G Ab Bb C	C Eb G Bb
C– or C–b6	Pure or Natural Minor, Aeolian	W H W W H W W	C D Eb F G Ab Bb C	C Eb G Bb
4. HALF DIMINISHED SCALE CHOICES	**SCALE NAME**	**W & H CONSTRUCTION**	**SCALE IN KEY OF C**	**BASIC CHORD IN KEY OF C**
CØ	Half Diminished (Locrian)	H W W H W W W	C Db Eb F Gb Ab Bb C	C Eb Gb Bb D
CØ2 (CØ9)	Half Diminished #2 (Locrian #2)	W H W H W W W	C D Eb F Gb Ab Bb C	C Eb Gb Bb D
CØ (with or without +2)	Bebop Scale	H W W H H H W W	C Db Eb F Gb Ab Bb C	C Eb Gb Bb
5. DIMINISHED SCALE CHOICES	**SCALE NAME**	**W & H CONSTRUCTION**	**SCALE IN KEY OF C**	**BASIC CHORD IN KEY OF C**
C°	Diminished (8 tone scale)	W H W H W H W H	C D Eb F Gb Ab A C	C Eb Gb A

INTRODUCTION TO THE SCALE SYLLABUS

Each chord/scale symbol (C7, C–, C△+4, etc.) represents a series of tones which the improvisor can use when improvising or soloing. These series of tones have traditionally been called scales. The scales listed here are the ones I most often hear musicians play. I have listed the Scale Syllabus in the key of C Concert so you can have a frame of reference and can compare the similarities and differences between the various chords/scales.

This SCALE SYLLABUS is intended to give the improvisor a variety of scale choices which may be used over any chord - major, minor, dominant 7th, half-diminished, diminished and suspended 4. Western music, especially jazz and pop, uses major, dominant 7th, Dorian minor and Blues scales and chords more than any other. Scales and chords used less often are the half-diminished, diminished and suspended 4. If we agree on these five basic scale families as being the most predominant, then we can set up categories and list substitute scales beneath each heading ... see the *Scale Syllabus* page. You should also check out **Volume 26 "The Scale Syllabus"** for more help with scales.

Each category begins with the scale most closely resembling the chord/scale symbol given to the left. The scales are arranged according to the degree of dissonance they produce in relation to the basic chord/scale sound. Scales near the top of each category will sound mild or consonant. Scale choices further down the list will become increasingly tense or dissonant. Each player is urged to start with the scales at the top and with practice and experimentation gradually work his way down the list to the more dissonant or tension-producing scales. You should work with a new scale sound on your instrument until your ears and fingers become comfortable with all the tones in the scale. Improvise with your voice over the scale you are learning and then reproduce on your instrument what your voice has created.

Music is made of tension and release. Scale tones produce either tension or relaxation. The improvisor's ability to control the amount and frequency of tension and release will, in large measure, determine whether he is successful in communicating to the listener. **Remember** - you, the player, are *also a listener!* Read **Volume 1 JAZZ: How To Play And Improvise** for a more detailed explanation of tension and release in melodic development.

Any of the various practice procedures and patterns listed in **Volumes 1, 2, 3, 21, 24 or 84** can be applied to any of the scale choices listed in this Scale Syllabus. Needless to say, any scale you want to learn should be transposed and practiced in all twelve keys. The column on whole and half step construction should prove helpful when transposing a scale to any of the twelve keys.

For additional information on scale substitution, I recommend *Scales for Jazz Improvisation* by Dan Haerle, **Jazz Improvisation** by David Baker, *Patterns for Jazz* (Treble-Clef or Bass Clef) and **Complete Method for Jazz Improvisation** by Jerry Coker, and *Repository of Scales & Melodic Patterns* by Yusef Lateef. These books are available from your favorite music source or visit www.jazzbooks.com for more information.

Several Play-A-Long sets offer you an opportunity to practice the various scales in all twelve keys. They are: *Vol. 24 Major & Minor; Vol. 84 Dominant 7th Workout; Vol.21 Gettin' It Together;* and *Vol.16 Turnarounds, Cycles & II/V7's.* You might also check out the Play-A-Longs which have tunes in all keys: *Vol. 42 Blues In All Keys; Vol. 47 Rhythm In All Keys; Vol. 57 Minor Blues In All Keys;* and two more volumes, *Vol. 67 Tune Up* and *Vol. 68 Giant Steps* - each has several classic tunes in all twelve keys.

Scales and chords are the backbone of our music and the better you equip yourself, the more fun you will have playing music.

NOTES: 1) The above chord symbol guide is my system of notation. I feel it best represents the sounds I hear in jazz. Players should be aware that each chord symbol represents a series of tones called a scale. **2)** Even though a C7+9 would appear to have only a raised 9th, it also has a b9, +4 and +5. The entire C7+9 scale looks like: Root, b9, +9, 3rd, +4, +5, b7 & root (C, Db, D#, E, F#, G#, Bb, C). My chord symbol C7+9 is therefore an abbreviation, while the complete name of this scale is Diminished Whole Tone (sometimes called Super Locrian or Altered Scale). Similarly, C7b9 also appears to have only one altered tone (b9) but it actually has three: b9, +9 and +4. The entire scale looks like: Root, b9, +9, 3rd, +4, 5th, 6th, b7 & root (C, Db, D#, E, F#, G, A, Bb, C). This is called a Diminished scale and my chord symbol is C7b9. **3)** All scales under the Dominant 7th category are scales that embellish the basic Dominant 7th sound. Some scales provide much more tension than the basic dominant 7th sound and require practice and patience to grasp the essence of their meaning. I encourage you to work with **Volume 3 "The 11-V7-1 Progression"** since it emphasizes Diminished and Diminished Whole Tone scales and chords. **4)** In category #3, MINOR SCALE CHOICES, the PURE MINOR scale choice is not used very often. I have found the order of preference to be Dorian, Bebop, Melodic, Blues, Pentatonic, and then any of the remaining Minor scale choices.

5

EXERCISE FOR PLAIN OLD TURNAROUND

The examples below are in four keys, C, Db, D, and Eb. You should practice this chord/scale progression in the other eight keys. You may wish to write out phrases yourself and then try playing the phrase throughout all twelve keys.

CD #1, Track 2

REMEMBER, the tonic scale can be improvised on for eight bars. The tonic scale is the first scale of each eight-bar section.

EXERCISE FOR TURNAROUND No. 2

CD #1, Track 3 (The small numbers beneath the notes indicate the scale tone)

6B

EXERCISE FOR TURNAROUND No. 3

CD #1, Track 4

EXERCISE FOR TURNAROUND No. 3
(melodic connecting)

This example is only written in one key - the Key of C. The 4th of the Db7 is usually raised ½ step. The Db7 chord/scale is called a "Neapolitan" chord /scale.

6D

CD #1, Track 5

This page of examples is written in one key.

EXERCISE FOR PLAIN OLD TURNAROUND

The examples below are in four keys, D, Eb, E, and F. You should practice this chord/scale progression in the other eight keys. You may wish to write out phrases yourself and then try playing the phrase throughout all twelve keys.

CD #1, Track 2

REMEMBER, the tonic scale can be improvised on for eight bars. The tonic scale is the first scale of each eight-bar section.

EXERCISE FOR TURNAROUND No. 2

(The small numbers beneath the notes indicate the scale tone)

EXERCISE FOR TURNAROUND No. 3

EXERCISE FOR TURNAROUND No. 3
(melodic connecting)

This example is only written in one key - the Key of D. The 4th of the Eb7 is usually raised ½ step. The Eb7 chord/scale is called a "Neapolitan" chord /scale.

CD #1, Track 4

EXERCISE FOR TURNAROUND No. 4

This page of examples is written in one key.

EXERCISE FOR PLAIN OLD TURNAROUND

The examples below are in four keys, A, Bb, B, and C. You should practice this chord/scale progression in the other eight keys. You may wish to write out phrases yourself and then try playing the phrase throughout all twelve keys.

CD #1, Track 2

REMEMBER, the tonic scale can be improvised on for eight bars. The tonic scale is the first scale of each eight-bar section.

EXERCISE FOR TURNAROUND No. 2

(The small numbers beneath the notes indicate the scale tone)

8B

EXERCISE FOR TURNAROUND No. 3

CD #1, Track 4

EXERCISE FOR TURNAROUND No. 3
(melodic connecting)

This example is only written in one key - the Key of A. The 4th of the Bb7 is usually
raised ½ step. The Bb7 chord/scale is called a "Neapolitan" chord /scale.

CD #1, Track 4

8D

EXERCISE FOR TURNAROUND No. 4
This page of examples is written in one key.

EXERCISE FOR PLAIN OLD TURNAROUND

The examples below are in four keys, C, Db, D, and Eb. You should practice this chord/scale progression in the other eight keys. You may wish to write out phrases yourself and then try playing the phrase throughout all twelve keys.

CD #1, Track 2

REMEMBER, the tonic scale can be improvised on for eight bars. The tonic scale is the first scale of each eight-bar section.

EXERCISE FOR TURNAROUND No. 2

(The small numbers beneath the notes indicate the scale tone)

CD #1, Track 3

9B

EXERCISE FOR TURNAROUND No. 3

EXERCISE FOR TURNAROUND No. 3
(melodic connecting)

This example is only written in one key - the Key of C. The 4th of the Db7 is usually raised ½ step. The Db7 chord/scale is called a "Neapolitan" chord /scale.

EXERCISE FOR TURNAROUND No. 4

This page of examples is written in one key.

9E

PLAIN OLD TURNAROUND No. 1
(1x)

CD #1, Track 2

TURNAROUNDS No. 2
(1x)

11

TURNAROUNDS No. 3

(1x)

TURNAROUNDS No. 4

(1x)

BALLAD II/V7/I
(1x)

A
D- G7 C△ | B- E7 A△ | Bb- Eb7 Ab△ | A- D7 G△

F- Bb7 Eb△ | F#- B7 E△ | E- A7 D△ | G- C7 F△

Eb- Ab7 Db△ | Ab- Db7 Gb△ | C- F7 Bb△ | C#- F#7 B△

B
D- G7 C- | B- E7 A- | Bb- Eb7 Ab- | A- D7 G-

F- Bb7 Eb- | F#- B7 E- | E- A7 D- | G- C7 F-

Eb- Ab7 Db- | Ab- Db7 Gb- | C- F7 Bb- | C#- F#7 B-

C
Dø G7+9 C- | Bø E7+9 A- | Bbø Eb7+9 Ab- | Aø D7+9 G-

Fø Bb7+9 Eb- | F#ø B7+9 E- | Eø A7+9 D- | Gø C7+9 F-

Ebø Ab7+9 Db- | Abø Db7+9 Gb- | Cø F7+9 Bb- | C#ø F#7+9 B-/E

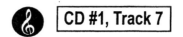

HALE BOP

By Jamey Aebersold

HALE BOP

CYCLES No. 1 (2 bars each)
(6x)

CD #1, Track 8

CYCLES No. 2 (1 bar each)
(7x)

CD #1, Track 9

CYCLES, No. 3 (2 beats each)
(10x)

CD #1, Track 10

CYCLES No. 4 fast tempo
(6x)

CD #1, Track 11

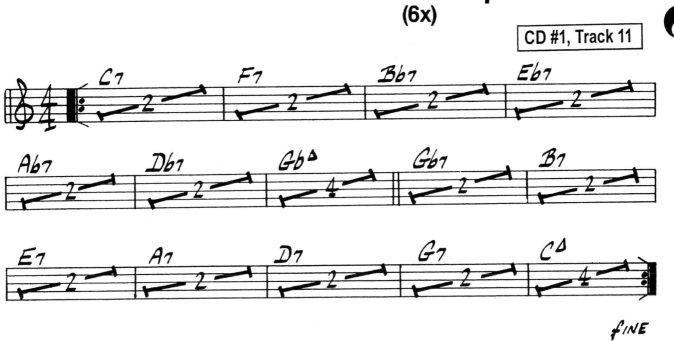

fine

CYCLES No. 5 fast tempo
(9x)

CD #1, Track 12

fine

V7+ 9/I (1 bar each)
(1x)

II/V7/I MAJOR — swing tempo

CD #2, Track 2

(1x)

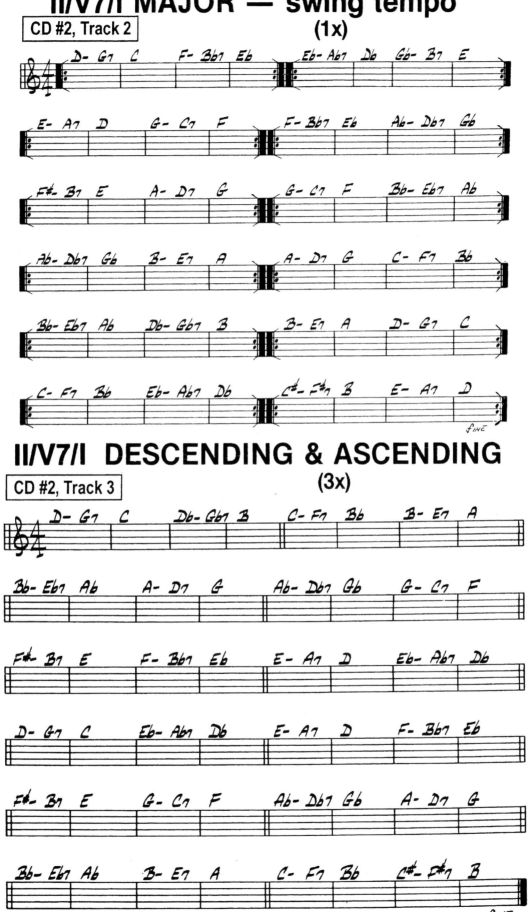

II/V7/I DESCENDING & ASCENDING

CD #2, Track 3

(3x)

II/V7 II/V7 II/V7/I
(1x)

D- G7 Eb- Ab7 E- A7 D | Eb- Ab7 E- A7 F- Bb7 Eb

E- A7 F- Bb7 F#- B7 E | F- Bb7 F#- B7 G- C7 F

F#- B7 G- C7 Ab- Db7 F# | G- C7 Ab- Db7 A- D7 G

Ab- Db7 A- D7 Bb- Eb7 Ab | A- D7 Bb- Eb7 B- E7 A

Bb- Eb7 B- E7 C- F7 Bb | B- E7 C- F7 C#- F#7 B

C- F7 C#- F#7 D- G7 C | C#- F#7 D- G7 Eb- Ab7 Db

Db- Gb7 C- F7 B- E7 A | C- F7 B- E7 Bb- Eb7 Ab

B- E7 Bb- Eb7 A- D7 G | Bb- Eb7 A- D7 Ab- Db7 Gb

A- D7 Ab- Db7 G- C7 F | Ab- Db7 G- C7 F#- B7 E

G- C7 F#- B7 F- Bb7 Eb | F#- B7 F- Bb7 E- A7 D

F- Bb7 E- A7 Eb- Ab7 Db | E- A7 Eb- Ab7 D- G7 C

Eb- Ab7 D- G7 Db- Gb7 B | D- G7 C#- F#7 C- F7 Bb

TRITONE SUBSTITUTES & IV/bVII/I
(1x)

COLTRANE CHANGES
(1x)

TURNAROUNDS FINAL

(1X)

Bb RHYTHM CHANGES

(4X)

COLTRANE BLUES

(11X)

26

SOME OF THE THINGS I AM

CD #2, Track 11

(5X)

GUESS WHAT KEY I'M IN (by Matt Eve)

CD #2, Track 12

(9X)

PLAIN OLD TURNAROUND No. 1
(1x)

TURNAROUNDS No. 2

(1x)

29

TURNAROUNDS No. 3
(1x)

CD #1, Track 4

TURNAROUNDS No. 4
(1x)

CD #1, Track 5

BALLAD II/V7/I
(1x)

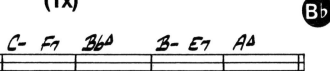

HALE BOP

By Jamey Aebersold

CYCLES No. 1 (2 bars each)
(6x)

Bb

CYCLES No. 2 (1 bar each)
(7x)

CYCLES, No. 3 (2 beats each)
(10x)

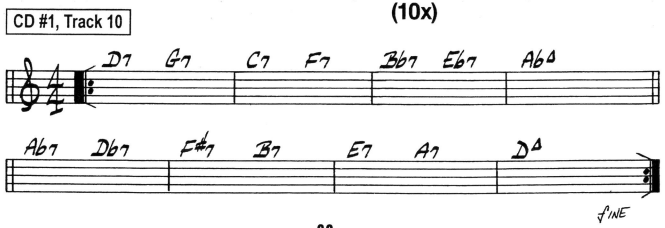

fine

CYCLES No. 4 fast tempo
(6x)

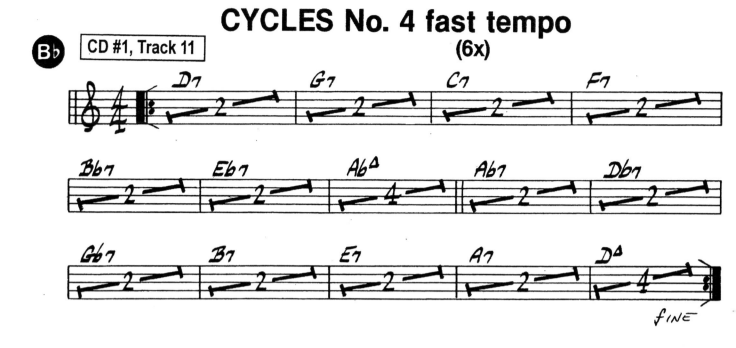

CYCLES No. 5 fast tempo
(9x)

34

V7 + 9/I (1 bar each)
(1x)

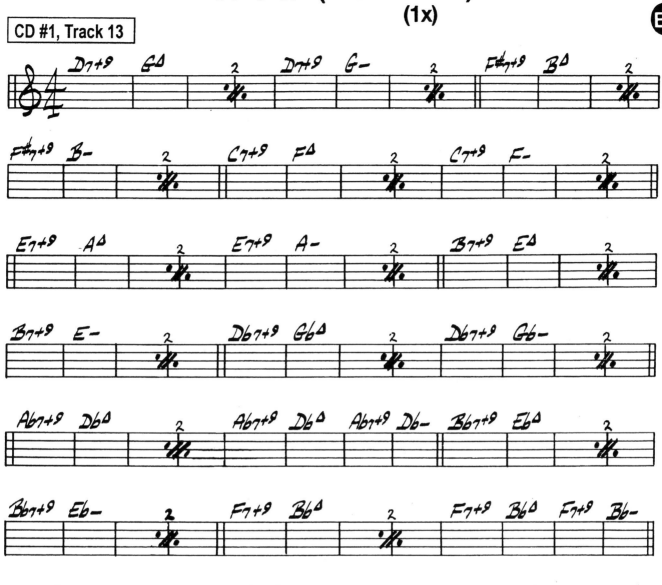

II/V7/I MAJOR — swing tempo

CD #2, Track 2

(1x)

IV/V7/I DESCENDING & ASCENDING

(3x)

CD #2, Track 3

36

II/V7   II/V7   II/V7/I

CD #2, Track 4   (1X)

fine

TRITONE SUBSTITUTES & IV/bVII/I
(1x)

Bb

G- C7 Db- Gb7 F | A- D7+9 G- C7 Bb- Eb7 F | %

E- A7 Bb- Eb7 D | F#- B7+9 E- A7 G- C7 D | %

C- F7 F#- B7 Bb | D- G7+9 C- F7 Eb- Ab7 Bb | %

Db- Gb7 G- C7 B | Eb- Ab7+9 Db- Gb7 E- A7 B | %

Bb- Eb7 E- A7 Ab | C- F7+9 Bb- Eb7 Db- Gb7 Ab | %

D- G7 Ab- Db7 C | E- A7+9 D- G7 F- Bb7 C | %

B- E7 F- Bb7 A | Db- Gb7+9 B- E7 D- G7 A | %

Ab- Db7 D- G7 F# | Bb- Eb7+9 Ab- Db7 B- E7 F# | %

F- Bb7 B- E7 Eb | G- C7+9 F- Bb7 Ab- Db7 Eb | %

F#- B7 C- F7 E | Ab- Db7+9 F#- B7 A- D7 E | %

Eb- Ab7 A- D7 Db△ | F- Bb7+9 Eb- Ab7 F#- B7 Db△ | %

A- D7 Eb- Ab7 G△ | B- E7+9 A- D7 C- F7 G△ |

COLTRANE CHANGES
(1x)

40

TURNAROUNDS FINAL
(1x)

B♭

Cont. next page....

RHYTHM CHANGES
(4x)

B♭

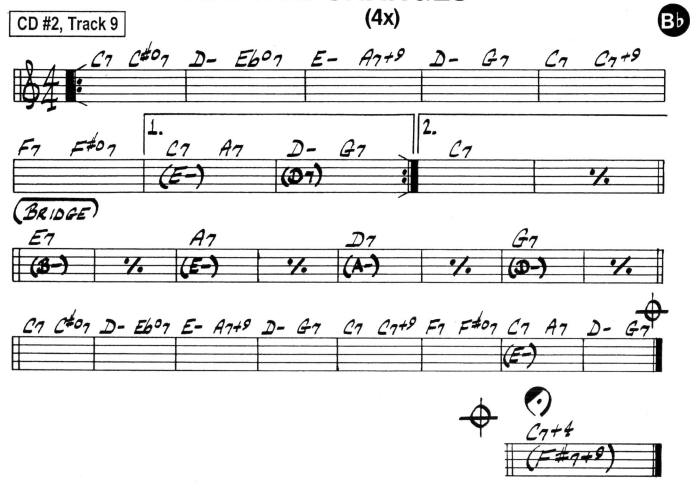

COLTRANE BLUES
(11x)

SOME OF THE THINGS I AM

(5X)

GUESS WHAT KEY I'M IN (by Matt Eve)

(9X)

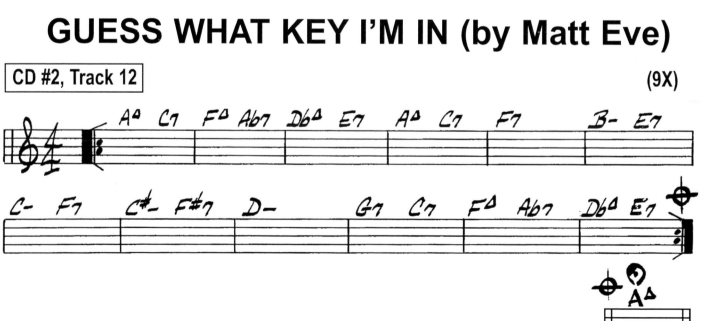

PLAIN OLD TURNAROUND No. 1

(1X)

TURNAROUNDS No. 2

(1x)

TURNAROUNDS No. 3
(1x)

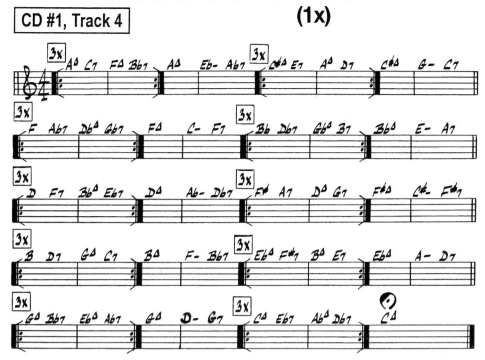

TURNAROUNDS No. 4
(1x)

BALLAD II/V7/I
(1x)

HALE BOP

Play 4 Times

CD #1, Track 7

Bossa Nova

By Jamey Aebersold

CYCLES No. 1 (2 bars each)
(6x)

CYCLES No. 2 (1 bar each)
(7x)

CYCLES, No. 3 (2 beats each)
(10x)

CYCLES No. 4 fast tempo
(6x)

CD #1, Track 11

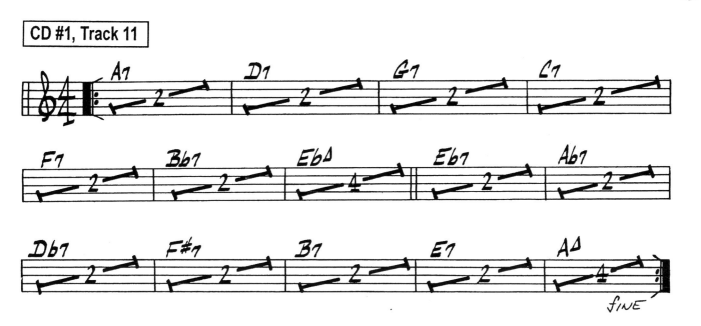

CYCLES No. 5 fast tempo
(9x)

CD #1, Track 12

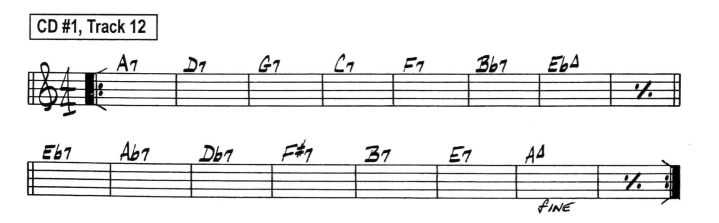

V7+ 9/I (1 bar each)
(1x)

II/V7/I MAJOR — swing tempo
(1x)

CD #2, Track 2

fine

IV/V7/I DESCENDING & ASCENDING
(3x)

CD #2, Track 3

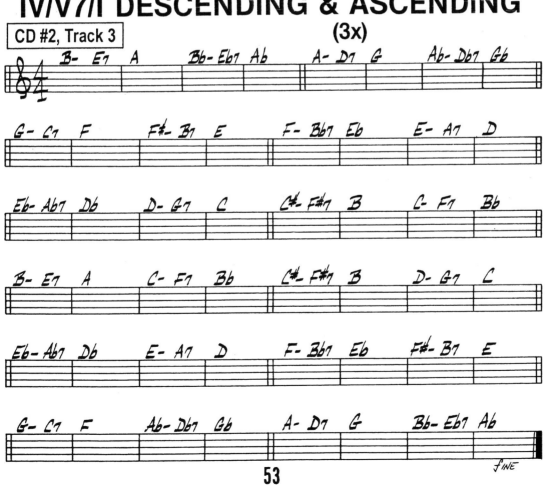

fine

53

II/V7 III/VI II/V7 III/VI II/V7 III/VI II/V7/I
(1x)

CD #2, Track 5

Eb

fine

TRITONE SUBSTITUTES & IV/bVII/I

(1x)

D- G7 | Ab- Db7 | C | E- A7+9 | D- G7 | F- Bb7 | C | ℅

B- E7 | F- Bb7 | A | C#- F#7+9 | B- E7 | D- G7 | A | ℅

G- C7 | C#- F#7 | F | A- D7+9 | G- C7 | Bb- Eb7 | F | ℅

Ab- Db7 | D- G7 | Gb | Bb- Eb7+9 | Ab- Db7 | B- E7 | F# | ℅

F- Bb7 | B- E7 | Eb | G- C7+9 | F- Bb7 | Ab- Db7 | Eb | ℅

A- D7 | Eb- Ab7 | G | B- E7+9 | A- D7 | C- F7 | G | ℅

F#- B7 | C- F7 | E | Ab- Db7+9 | F#- B7 | A- D7 | E | ℅

Eb- Ab7 | A- D7 | Db | F- Bb7+9 | Eb- Ab7 | F#- B7 | Db | ℅

C- F7 | F#- B7 | Bb | D- G7+9 | C- F7 | Eb- Ab7 | Bb | ℅

Db- Gb7 | G- C7 | B | Eb- Ab7+9 | Db- Gb7 | E- A7 | B | ℅

Bb- Eb7 | E- A7 | Ab | C- F7+9 | Bb- Eb7 | Db- Gb7 | Ab | ℅

E- A7 | Bb- Eb7 | D | F#- B7+9 | E- A7 | G- C7 | DΔ

COLTRANE CHANGES
(1x)

57

TURNAROUNDS FINAL
(1x)

RHYTHM CHANGES
(4x)

CD #2, Track 9

COLTRANE BLUES
(11x)

CD #2, Track 10

60

SOME OF THE THINGS I AM

(5X)

GUESS WHAT KEY I'M IN (by Matt Eve)

CD #2, Track 12

(9X)

NOTE ABOUT THE VOL. 16 CDs

There are FOUR CDs with the Vol. 16 Play-A-Long

Both CD#1 and CD#2 include SLOWER and FASTER tempo editions. It is recommended that you start with the slower tempo CDs and then to move onto the faster tempo CDs when comfortable.